Mindfulness Activities
for Kids with ADHD

This Book Belongs to:

....

Mindfulness Activities for Kids with ADHD

ENGAGING STORIES AND EXERCISES TO HELP YOU LEARN AND THRIVE

SHARON GRAND, PhD

Illustrations by Taia Morley

ROCKRIDGE
PRESS

For general information on our other products and services or to obtain technical support, please contact our Customer Care Department within the United States at (866) 744-2665, or outside the United States at (510) 253-0500.

Rockridge Press publishes its books in a variety of electronic and print formats. Some content that appears in print may not be available in electronic books, and vice versa.

Interior and Cover Designer: Patricia Fabricant
Art Producer: Tom Hood
Editors: Marisa A. Hines and Nora Spiegel
Production Editor: Mia Moran
Production Manager: Riley Hoffman
Illustrations © Taia Morley 2021

ISBN: Print 978-1-64876-633-6 | eBook 978-1-64876-137-9
R0

To Josh, who led us in the ADHD
adventure, and to Brenden,
my partner and champion along
the way.

Contents

A Note to Parents and Caregivers

This book is designed with love and compassion for all families and children living with attention deficit hyperactivity disorder (ADHD). If your child has been diagnosed with ADHD, you may be reading this now in an attempt to understand how your intelligent, energetic, talented, and deeply loving child may struggle with basic undertakings as simple as paying attention, listening, sitting still, remaining calm, staying organized, or completing tasks independently. This book takes you and your child through a course of gentle education, with stories and exercises to guide you along the way.

ADHD is a neurological condition that affects the parts of our brain responsible for self-control, organization, planning, attention, and memory, among others. When a child struggles with these types of executive functions, you might see that they have difficulty initiating tasks, staying organized, sustaining attention, managing time, shifting focus, or controlling their emotions. Children may struggle with tasks that require sustained attention, such as schoolwork, but when engaging with something they enjoy, they may have the ability to become extremely and effortlessly focused, even if the task may seem difficult to us.

Mindfulness is a wonderful tool that teaches us how to observe ourselves and find focus. It has been shown to be important for children with ADHD, as it improves their ability to self-observe, train their attention, reduce impulsivity, and cope with stressful experiences. Of course, there are many other critical supports to consider, including nutrition, sleep, psychotherapy, neurofeedback, educational interventions, and medical evaluations. Please check out the "Resources" section (page 114) for more information.

Whether your child has ADHD or they are just struggling with some of the signs and symptoms, I hope this book will encourage them to share their experiences with you. In this book, three stories follow the adventures of animal friends experiencing some of the diverse signs of ADHD. For example, Fig the bird is high energy, fast talking, impulsive, and hyper-focused on bugs. Fern the fox is more of a "daydreamer," easily distracted and overwhelmed by her environment, and she can get lost in her own thoughts.

Woven through the stories, you'll find a variety of mindfulness activities to help your child learn skills and techniques to manage their ADHD and questions sprinkled in to bolster your child's understanding of their own experiences. At the end, we'll conclude with a recap of some of the most important techniques and how you and your child can incorporate them into your everyday life plus a fun opportunity for your child to show you (and quiz you on!) what they've learned.

This book was designed to grow with your child. "Smart as a Fox, Clever as a Bird!" is for very young children, and "The 'Tail' of Two Lucys" and "Billie Jean, the *Drama Queen*?" grow a bit more complex for older kids. Read the stories ahead of time to be prepared and go at your child's pace to engage with the material. These stories and exercises are intended to help your child feel great, increase calm focus, embrace their unique strengths, and understand that they are not alone. Best of all, you and your child will benefit from the special time you spend reading these stories and practicing the techniques together.

A Note to Kids

What is ADHD? ADHD can mean a lot of different things, but it all relates to how your brain and body work together. Maybe you tend to think about lots of different things instead of one thing at a time. Maybe your body finds it easier to go fast than slow. Maybe you need help remembering to do things because your mind is so busy with all your thoughts or daydreams. Some kids with ADHD may have to work harder on skills like paying attention, being on time, or staying calm. On the other hand, kids with ADHD typically excel at curiosity, creativity, imagination, and kindness.

Everyone has some skills that come easily and has to work harder at others. Someone might be great at basketball and struggle with math. It does not mean they cannot do math; it just means they may have to use more effort.

What is mindfulness, and how does it help with ADHD? Mindfulness is about noticing what is happening right now. When you notice what is happening around you, you are better able to focus. This helps you calm down if you are sad or frustrated. It also helps with school, sports, and friendships because we all do better when we pay attention.

Did you know that a person with ADHD can do anything they choose? In fact, many have chosen to do very cool things like becoming movie stars, scientists, and even billionaires! This book will teach you how helpful mindfulness can be for ADHD and for everyday life. I hope you have fun with the activities and learn a lot. Always remember . . . you are smart as a fox, clever as a bird. You can be as silly as a puppy or as sweet as a bunny. And you are definitely as cool as a Chihuahua!

SMART as a FOX, CLEVER as a BIRD!

Fig's Fall

Fig lived in a nest high up in a tree. One day he fell out of the nest, away from his squawky siblings, through the green leaves, until—*bump!*—he landed on the soft earth below.

He yelled, but his mother did not hear. He hopped and flapped, but his brothers and sisters did not see. "What will I do now?" he wondered.

"Hey," said a friendly fox. "I'm Fern. Why are you here on the ground?"

"I fell down," said Fig. He wanted to go home. Fig was lost and scared in the big forest.

Fern picked up a feather. "Watch this." She took a big breath and blew. "Look at it flutter!"

Fig looked only at the feather. He breathed in and blew out toward the feather. It fluttered again!

Fig wondered how long he could make the feather flutter. He blew slowly and counted "1, 2, 3, 4, 5" in his mind. He tried again for longer and counted "1, 2, 3, 4, 5, 6, 7, 8, 9, 10."

His mind grew quiet and clear. Then Fig saw the way home!

"Fern, help me up to that branch. I know how to get back to my nest!"

QUESTIONS:

→ Fig had an unexpected adventure when he fell from his nest. Have you ever been on an unexpected adventure?

→ Fern helped Fig feel better. Who helps you feel better?

→ Fig used feather breathing to calm him. Can you do feather flutter breathing too?

ACTIVITY:
Feather Flutter Breathing

Hold a feather in front of you and look at it. Focus on the feather.

Place your other hand on your belly. Take a deep breath and feel your belly get big.

Blow out slowly on the feather. Feel your belly get small. Can you make the feather flutter?

How long can you make the feather flutter?

Can you make the feather flutter with your nose?

Fern's Den

Fig was happy to be going to Fern's house today.

"I'm going to Fern's," he said, skipping past Anne. "To play in her den," he chirped, twirling around the twins Mac and Mia.

"Watch out, Fig!" squawked Pixel, the oldest sibling. "You almost knocked me over!"

"Sorry," said Fig.

Mama laughed. "Fig, you may fall out of the nest and right into your playdate."

"I did that last time!" said Fig.

Fig flew down and found Fern waiting for Fig in her den. "Hello, Fig. Come in! Come in!"

Fern's den was big and brown. It was quiet and deep and smelled like the earth.

Fern and Fig sat on her big comfy pillow and nibbled on a new snack: wild berries. There were little red ones, round blue ones, and big purple ones. The berries were sweet and tart. Yum!

They ate them slowly, one by one, until soon there were no more.

Fig remembered that Anne liked berries. So did Mac and Mia and even Pixel too.

"Fern," said Fig, "are there any more berries?"

"We can pick more in the forest. Let's go!"

QUESTIONS:

- Fig skips and twirls when he is happy. What do you do when you are happy?

- Fern's den is brown and quiet. What are the colors and sounds in your home?

- Fern's den smells like the earth. What do you like to smell?

ACTIVITY: Wild Berry Challenge

Find a "wild" berry in your refrigerator, like a blueberry, strawberry, or blackberry. Let's observe it.

What shape is the berry?

Is it smooth or bumpy?

What color is it?

Take a little nibble. What does it taste like?

Challenge yourself to eat the berry very slowly. Make it last as long as possible and enjoy every bite!

Into the Forest

Fig and Fern skipped into the forest. Fern brought two buckets, one for each of the friends to fill with berries. But how would they find the berries?

Fig flew up and down and zigzagged all around. His mind was full of questions. "Is this a wild berry?" he asked Fern. "Where are they hiding? Up here? Down there? Where could they be?"

Fern did not answer. She forgot to listen, and she forgot to look for berries. She was busy daydreaming about wild berry pie.

"Listen, Fern, listen," Fig chirped and hopped all around her. "Let's play a game while we walk through the forest. Let's look and find three things we can see. Let's listen and find two things we can hear. Let's focus and find one thing we can feel."

Fern and Fig looked all around the big, green forest.

"Look," said Fern, "a mushroom!"

"I see!" said Fig. "And I found a stone!"

The two friends saw mushrooms, stones, and branches.
They heard birds and squirrels. They closed their eyes.
They felt the soft wind blow.

ACTIVITY: Forest Name Game

Pick a spot to play. You can play anywhere.

Look around. Can you name three things you can see? Fern and Fig found mushrooms, stones, and branches in the forest.

Listen carefully. What do you hear? Birds? People? Name two things you can hear.

Notice your body. What do you feel? The warm sun? The soft carpet under your feet? Name one thing you can feel.

Bugs and Trees

"I like this name game!" chirped Fig. "Let's play again.
Look, Fern, I found a wiggly worm. Worms are slimy.
Did you know that, Fern?"

"Eww!" said Fern, stepping away.

"I love worms," chirped Fig happily. "And insects too.
I know a lot about them. Did you know that bees have hair
on their eyeballs?"

"Oh," said Fern. She did NOT like bugs.

"Spiders make sticky webs to catch bugs," said Fig,
pretending to be stuck in a web. "Isn't that funny, Fern?"

But Fern didn't hear. She wanted to play a new game.
A game without bugs. Fern planted her back paws firmly on
the ground. She reached her front paws way up in the air.
"Look, Fig!" she said. "I'm a tree. Can you pretend to be a
tree like me?"

Fig stopped and wondered what it was like to be a tree.
He imagined his feet were the roots. He pretended his
wings were branches and his feathers were leaves. Fig took
a deep breath of the forest air. He stood like a tree, calm
and quiet. Being a tree made Fig feel strong.

QUESTIONS:

→ Fig loves insects! He knows a lot about them! What is something you know a lot about?

→ Do you think Fern likes bugs?

→ How do you know what Fern was feeling?

→ What do you think is yucky?

ACTIVITY: Tree Pose

Would you like to pose like a tree?

Plant your right foot firmly on the floor, like the root of a tree.

Place the ball of your left foot on the ground and the heel on your right ankle.

Bring your hands together at your heart; then reach up for the sky!

Imagine the sun is shining in the forest.

Feel calm and relaxed.

Feel quiet and strong.

Like a Ladybug

"I'm a tree! I'm a tree!" Fig chirped to Fern.

First, Fig posed like a giant elm with wings up toward the sky. Then he posed like a weeping willow with wings drooping down to the ground.

"Look at me, Fern! Watch me be a tree."

Fern was not watching Fig. His voice was small, and Fern's thoughts were big. She wanted to be a tree, but she didn't want ANY icky bugs crawling on her!

"What are you doing?" asked Fig.

"Watching for bugs," said Fern.

"Oh," said Fig. "I'll help you."

Fig found a honeybee on a yellow flower. *Buzz buzz!*
Fig saw a ladybug on a green leaf. *Wiggle and freeze.*
Fig giggled. The ladybug was funny. *Wiggle and freeze.*
Fig started wiggling too.

"Look, Fern, I'm a ladybug!"

Fern laughed. The ladybug wasn't scary or gross. "I want to play too!" *Wiggle and freeze.* Fern felt her body move all about. She felt her breath go in and out. *Wiggle and freeze.* Fern was happy. It's fun to be a ladybug!

QUESTIONS:

→ Fern's thoughts were so big she could not watch Fig at all! Do you ever have big thoughts?

→ What kind of bug would you want to be?

→ Fern felt happy when she moved all about! How do you move all about?

ACTIVITY: Wiggle and Freeze

Are you ready to move like a ladybug?

Think of the word "Go!" and move your body all around!

Wiggle around for a few seconds until you think the word "Freeze!"

Freeze for a few seconds.

Hold very still.

Feel the quiet.

Ready, set, go again!

VARIATIONS

Musical freeze game: Dance while the music is on, and freeze when it turns off!

Breathing freeze: While frozen, take a deep breath in and a slow breath out; then go!

The Bamboo Forest

Fig and Fern followed the ladybug through the forest. The forest was filled with colors and sounds and bright scents.

"Look, Fig," said Fern. "Another ladybug! And another!" Fern liked bugs now . . . well, some of them.

Fern and Fig watched as more and more ladybugs came out to greet them. Ladybugs twirling and ladybugs flying. Fern and Fig danced with the ladybugs until they were out of breath.

One by one the ladybugs disappeared into the forest. Fig looked up. He could not see the path anymore, and bamboo grew high all around them. They were lost!

"Help! Help!" he cried, as he fluttered, jumped, and looked for the path. The bamboo beneath his feet made a noise as he hopped about. Fern liked the sound. She picked up two bamboo sticks and hit them together.

"Fig . . . listen." *Plunk!*

Fig listened. The sound started loud and grew softer, and then Fig could not hear it at all. *Plunk!* Fig's mind grew quiet with the sound. The two friends sat calmly together, safe in the bamboo forest.

QUESTIONS:

→ Have you ever been scared?

→ When Fig was scared, his mind got noisy. Fern used bamboo sticks to help calm Fig's mind. What do you like to do to help calm your mind?

ACTIVITY: Chimes

This activity can be done with an instrument like a xylophone, drum, or chime that makes a long sound.

Find a comfortable position in a quiet place.

Take a deep breath in, and slowly breathe out.

Relax your muscles from head to toe.

Play a sound on the instrument.

Listen to the sound start loud and then get softer until it is gone.

When you can no longer hear it, raise your hand.

Fern's Tail

Fern sniffed around the bamboo forest looking for the trail. Fern's strong nose smelled flowers, mold, and mushrooms. Her bright eyes saw frogs, leaves, and rocks. Fern looked all around but did not find the trail. She grew scared, and her heart beat faster. Her body and mind spun in circles.

"Where is the trail?" Fern wondered. "Where are the berries? How do we go home?" Fern could not think at all. Fig followed Fern as she walked in circles. He was getting dizzy.

"Stop, Fern!"

Fern stopped walking. Her body was still, but her tail kept moving. Back and forth, round and round. They both watched quietly, and soon Fern's tail started to slow. Fern's tail was just like Fern's feelings. When her feelings were strong and fast, her tail moved strong and fast. When her feelings were soft and slow, her tail moved soft and slow.

Fern slowed her tail down little by little. Her mind slowed down too, and when her tail stopped spinning, Fern felt quiet and calm.

QUESTIONS:

➔ Fern was so frightened that her mind was spinning! Do you ever remember a time when your mind was spinning?

➔ Fig and Fern grew calm when they focused on Fern's tail. How does your body or your breath change as you become calmer?

ACTIVITY: Foxtail

Have an adult cut a piece of yarn about 12 inches long and tie a button on the end.

Hold the other end and spin the button round and round.

Freeze your hand and watch the string spin slower and slower until it stops.

Allow your thoughts and feelings to slow with the movement of the string until it stops and you feel calm and clear.

Where Are the Wild Berries?

"Fern," said Fig, "what if we never find the wild berries? What if it is too hard?"

"Fig," said Fern, "we can do it. Let's keep trying."

"Yes, Fern," said Fig. "We found mushrooms, trees, ladybugs, and bamboo. We are good at finding, but wild berries are good at hiding."

Fern smiled and said, "The forest knows where the wild berries are. Listen! The forest speaks, and we can hear it. Be silent and still as a tree. Let your eyes look. Let your ears listen. Feel your chest rise and fall like the waves of the ocean. Let your thoughts blow away like the clouds in the sky."

Fern was silent and still as a tree. Her senses grew strong, and her mind was as clear as the big, blue sky. She listened to the buzzing bees and watched a ladybug crawl. *Wiggle and freeze.* Suddenly, Fern remembered seeing purple, juicy berries peeking out. She saw them when her mind was busy playing wiggle and freeze.

"I know where the berries are! Let's go, Fig!"

➡️ Fig felt like they were never going to find the wild berries! Have you ever wanted to give up when something was too hard? What helped you keep trying?

➡️ Fern lost the path and forgot where the berries were. Have you ever lost something important? What did you do?

ACTIVITY: Silent as a Fox

Find a comfortable place to sit.

Place your hand on your chest and breathe. Feel it rise and fall like the ocean.

Be silent and still. Feel your breath move in and out.

Turn on your super senses.

Let your eyes see.

Let your ears listen.

Let your body feel.

Let your thoughts blow away like the clouds.

Let your mind grow clear.

Spread Your Wings

Fern remembered where the berries were, but she did not know how to get there. "I can't find the path on the ground," Fern said.

Fig knew he could see the path from the sky, but he was scared. He had never flown so high before. But Fig was also brave. He spread out his beautiful wings and began to fly. He flew over the branches to the top of the trees and burst out into the blue sky!

"Woo-hoo!" cried Fig.

Fig looked down and saw the forest below him. All was quiet and calm, and Fig felt at peace. From up here, he could easily see the path.

Fern walked through the forest by following Fig as he flew in the sky, and the two friends found their way out of the bamboo forest. One from above, one from below. They went over and under the trees, past the ladybugs, until they found wild berries peeking out from behind a bush.

Fig and Fern cheered. They ate wild berries and filled their buckets.

QUESTIONS:

➜ Fig was brave. Can you remember a time when you were brave?

➜ Fig and Fern solved the problem and found the wild berries! What do you like to get when you solve problems?

➜ Fig felt at peace in the sky. Where do you feel at peace?

ACTIVITY: Bird's-Eye View

Stand up tall and spread your arms like wings.

Keep your feet planted firmly on the floor.

Now, imagine yourself high in the sky and soaring through the air.

Feel the cool breeze.

Allow your body to feel safe and lifted.

Keep your mind as clear as the blue sky.

Look around you and let your eyes see everything in a different way.

The Way Home

Fig and Fern were ready to go home. The forest was growing dark, and their buckets were bursting with wild berries.

As they walked, Fig and Fern talked about all they had learned. Fern learned to watch mindfully. Fig learned to listen mindfully. Fern learned to be still and silent. Fig learned to fly high. Fern and Fig were the best of friends.

They reached a fork in the path. Which way should they go?

"Look, Fern," said Fig as he pointed at a set of muddy prints. "A fox and a bird. It's us! Follow me!"

Fern turned on her super senses, and her mind grew quiet. She looked only at the prints.

She tracked them step by step until the muddy prints brought Fern and Fig home to their families.

That night, Fern and her father made wild berry pie. Fig, Mama, Papa, Anne, Mac, Mia, and Pixel all came over to have some. It was scrumptious!

Fig and Fern sat under the stars to rest. Today's adventure was over, and they were full of joy.

"That was fun," said Fig.

"Let's do it again tomorrow!" said Fern.

QUESTIONS:

➡ Fern and Fig are the best of friends! Who are your very best friends?

➡ Fern and her father baked a pie to share. What do you like to share?

➡ Fern and Fig rested under the stars. What do you do at night to rest?

ACTIVITY:
Track Your Paw Prints Home

Connect the paw prints to follow Fig and Fern through their journey to find wild berries and return home.

The "TAIL" of TWO LUCYS

A New Paw Scout

"Welcome to Paw Scouts!" read the sign in the gym. Lucy Bunny felt timid, and she held on to her mother's hand. The gym was full of the sounds of laughing, shouting, and banging. Dozens of scouts wore bright vests in colors that showed their rank. Lucy Bunny wore her brown uniform with her name tag and her welcome pin that read "New Member."

The Eagle Scout in charge flew over—*whoosh!*—and startled Lucy Bunny. "Welcome, Lucy!" she said with a warm smile. "Please join the activities."

Lucy Bunny and her mom went outside and saw turtles raising tents, woodchucks chucking wood, and honey bears bearing honey.

"Watch out!!!" A puppy with golden fur almost crashed into Lucy Bunny and then smiled an apology. "I guess I'm not a great dancer." She pointed at Lucy Bunny's tag and then her own. "Hey," she said, "my name is Lucy too!"

Lucy Puppy returned to the group dancing in a circle of fireflies. Lucy Bunny was shy, but she wanted to dance. She remembered that her teacher had taught her a "bunny body scan" to help her feel calm and brave.

ACTIVITY:
Bunny Scan from Ear to Tail

1. Find a quiet place to sit or lie down. Place your hand on your belly and take three deep, slow breaths.

2. Feel your breath going into and out of your nose. Think about your eyes, nose, and mouth and notice how they feel. Allow them to relax.

3. Working downward, scan the rest of your body, one part at a time, all the way down to your toes. Notice if any part of your body feels hot, cold, relaxed, or restless. Allow each part to relax.

4. Allow yourself to feel calmer and more relaxed with every breath you take.

Lucy Meets Lucy

Lucy Puppy waved at Lucy Bunny from the dance floor. Lucy Bunny's mom kissed her goodbye, and Lucy Bunny bravely hopped over. Her nose twitched, her ears wiggled, and her tail bounced up and down. Hop left, hop right, two hops now! Lucy Puppy's tail wagged as she tried it too, and both Lucys laughed as they let themselves tumble, spin, and be silly.

The two Lucys ran to get a drink at the snack table. Lucy Puppy proudly pointed to one of the large honey bears.

"That's my dad," she said. "I'm adopted. I know it's hard to tell because we look just the same." She gave Lucy Bunny a grin to show that she was kidding.

Lucy Bunny showed Lucy Puppy her mother, a pretty brown bunny.

The two Lucys discovered they had a lot in common. They both loved arts and crafts and shared a love for their favorite pop star, DJ Draper, the Chi-hua-hua Wonder.

"I wish I could dance like you," said Lucy Puppy.

"I'll teach you," offered Lucy Bunny. "It's easy! You just take a few steps, and then you move your body with the music. First, you have to become aware of the music, so listen mindfully."

QUESTIONS:

→ The two Lucys like crafts and DJ Draper. What are some things you like?

→ The two Lucys have a lot in common. Do you know anyone who is a lot like you?

→ Lucy Bunny is a great dancer! What is something unique and special about you?

ACTIVITY:
Pay Attention to the Music

Put on some music. Close your eyes and listen quietly. Let go of your feelings about the song. You may like it or not. Just let your mind move with the sound of the music.

Can you hear all of the different instruments? Pay attention to one at a time and try to hear each play by itself.

When you are ready, tap your hand to the sound of the beat. If you want to, start dancing!

The Chi-hua-hua Wonder

The two Lucys closed their eyes. They held paws and listened to the music. Lucy Puppy noticed the rhythmic *bum-ba-bum* of the drums and the electric sounds of the keyboard. She opened her eyes and began tapping her paw. Before she knew it, she was dancing along with the music!

Suddenly, the speaker boomed throughout the gym. "It's the latest hit by DJ Draper, the Chi-hua-hua Wonder!"

Shouts filled the room as a bass guitar rose from a soft hum to a giant crescendo. Scouts from every corner ran to the dance floor. Woodchucks, badgers, and beavers bounced over, cats stole quietly out of the shadows, fireflies flew, and bats burst onto the scene.

"Here we go! Here we go!" the scouts shouted along with the lyrics. "Every puppy on the trail, shake your paw and chase your tail!" Even the grown-ups were bopping to the beat.

Lucy Puppy moved to the music. Lucy Bunny hopped all around her. The scouts were having one big party, and Lucy Bunny had never felt so happy!

QUESTIONS:

→ The two Lucys love the songs by DJ Draper! What are your favorite songs to dance to?

→ Sometimes it's great to have a place where you can let your body run, shout, wiggle, and move around as much as you like! Where can you just let yourself go?

ACTIVITY:
My Favorite Song and Me

Can you draw how you feel when listening to your favorite song? Take out your colored pencils or crayons and write the title of your favorite song in the frame on the next page. You can also write out some of the lyrics. Can you illustrate a time when you listened to your favorite song? How did it make you feel? Did you dance? Smile? Jump all around?

My favorite song:............................

....

Lucy Bunny's Thumping Paw

DJ Draper's song came to an end. "Okay, scouts! Lunchtime!" the Eagle Scout announced while flying overhead.

Lucy Bunny was still full of energy and wanted to keep dancing. But the music ended, and the scouts moved to the tables to eat lunch.

Lucy Bunny wanted to cooperate. She sat at the table with the others and tried to be quiet, but her paws wouldn't let her be still. They wanted to hop! Her ears wanted to wiggle! Her tail wanted to bounce! Her nose wanted to twitch!

"Be still," Lucy Bunny said to herself.

She took a deep breath and tried to keep her muscles tight so they wouldn't move. *Twitch!* went her nose. Lucy Bunny rubbed her nose with her paw and began crunching on a carrot. *Thump!* went her paw. Lucy Bunny willed her paw to stop. *Thump thump thump!* It kept moving. *Thump thump thump!* Lucy turned in her seat to hide the stubborn paw under the picnic table. She hoped no one would notice.

➡ Lucy Bunny is having a hard time keeping her body still. Have you ever had a hard time keeping your body still? Where were you?

➡ Lucy Bunny does not want the other scouts to see that her body is moving. Why do you think she might feel this way?

ACTIVITY:
Paws on the Ground

Stand up. Bring your attention all the way down to your feet on the ground. Breathe steadily. Let all of your muscles relax. Close your eyes and imagine yourself with roots, like a tree, that connect your feet deep into the ground. Notice your feet touching the ground, and let the ground help you feel strong, steady, and calm. Let the feeling of calm spread to your whole body.

Lucy Puppy's Mindful Trick

Thump thump thump! went Lucy Bunny's paw under the table. A few of the scouts heard the sound and wondered what was making the noise. Two cats who were slurping up milkshakes started to giggle. *Thump thump thump!* Lucy Bunny blushed as more animals began to notice the sounds of her uncooperative paw.

Lucy Puppy walked over to Lucy Bunny's table. "Hey," she said. "I have a surprise for you! Follow me."

Lucy Puppy took a pawful of animal crackers and led her friend to a quiet place. "I know another way that we are just alike. Your paw wants to keep on thumping. My tail wants to keep on wagging. During story time, my tail wags, hits my friends right in their noses, and makes them all sneeze. Once during quiet time, my tail knocked the pencil cup off the teacher's desk!"

Lucy Bunny had wanted to cry, but hearing Lucy Puppy's stories made her laugh instead.

"You are mindful when you dance," said Lucy Puppy. "You can be mindful anytime, even when you eat. Being mindful calms our bodies when it is time for us to stop moving. Do you want to try the Animal Crackers game with me?"

Lucy Bunny nodded gratefully.

QUESTIONS:

➔ Lucy Puppy helped Lucy Bunny feel better when she was embarrassed and sad. Who helps you feel better when you feel bad?

➔ Do you think it was nice for the cats to giggle at Lucy Bunny? Why or why not?

ACTIVITY: Animal Crackers

Hold an animal cracker in your hand.

Look at it. What animal is it?

Touch it. Does it feel smooth or rough?

Break off a piece. **Listen** to the sound it makes. Is the sound soft or crunchy?

Smell it. What does it smell like?

Take a small bite. Chew slowly and notice the **taste**.
Is it delicious? How does it feel in your mouth?
Take another bite and observe again.

A Mind Full of Carrots

Lucy Bunny felt better. She returned to the table with Lucy Puppy, and they happily munched on carrots, crackers, and other goodies. Lucy Puppy chatted about how fun it was to join the Paw Scouts.

"They have camping every month," Lucy Puppy said. "The turtles are going to teach me to pitch a tent, and I'm going to get lots of badges. What badges do you want, Lucy Bunny? I want to get camping, archery, and my art badge, of course."

Lucy Bunny wanted to listen to her friend. But the morning had been busy and exciting, and Lucy Bunny's mind began to wander. "Is there a baking badge?" she wondered. "I'm sure my mom would help me. What could I bake?" The carrots on the table looked tempting. Lucy Bunny's mind filled with visions of carrot cakes, carrot muffins, and sliced carrot coins overflowing in a treasure chest.

Lucy Bunny tried hard to listen to her friend, but her mind was full of carrots!

ACTIVITY:
Counting Carrots

Can you help Lucy Bunny find and count her carrots? Color them in as you find them.

Helping the Garden Gophers

When snack was over, the two Lucys helped the other scouts clean the table.

"Many hands make light work," the Eagle Scout chirped cheerfully. "Okay, scouts, let's go."

They ran out to a big field next to a river for even more activities. The turtles played games underneath big tents. Cat counselors were teaching the young scouts how to make arrows for archery, and beavers were demonstrating the use of a dam to water plants in a big, organic garden!

The two Lucys helped the garden gophers dig holes to plant basil, mint, and chives. Lucy Puppy was especially good at this.

"I usually dig plants *out* of the ground!" Lucy Puppy said happily. "It's fun to bury them instead."

The river babbled softly, the air smelled of fresh green grass, and the sun shone warmly. Lucy Bunny thought the garden was a perfect place to meditate just like her grandmother had taught her.

"Lucy Puppy," she said, "Let's close our eyes for a few minutes."

The two Lucys closed their eyes. They heard the river, smelled the herbs, felt the warm sun above and the cool ground below. The more they noticed, the better they felt!

QUESTIONS:

→ Lucy Puppy is good at digging! What are you good at?

→ The two Lucys closed their eyes to meditate. They noticed the sound of the river, the feel of the sun, and the smell of basil, mint, and chives. What do you notice when you close your eyes?

ACTIVITY:
Close Your Bunny Eyes: Meditation

Find a place to sit or lie down and close your eyes. **Breathe** steadily.

What do you **hear**? **Listen** closely to the sounds around you.

How does your body **feel**? Are your muscles relaxed or tight? Are you comfortable? Take a moment to get comfortable if you need to.

Keep breathing and **focus** on how you feel right now. If your thoughts wander, wrap each thought in a bubble and softly blow it away. Notice again your senses, your breath, and your body.

The Broken Basil

Lucy Bunny and Lucy Puppy sat in the sun with their eyes closed. It was peaceful and quiet.

"Watch out!" yelled a voice as something whizzed past Lucy Bunny's ear.

The friends opened their eyes and saw a bright blue Frisbee lying in the basil patch. Many of the little green plants were bent and broken, and Lucy Puppy's eyes filled with tears.

"Sorry!" said a young turtle as he picked up the Frisbee.

Lucy Bunny looked up and saw a kindly gopher heading their way with a trowel. "It's okay. Let's take a look," said the gopher. "Well, well. The basil will grow back just fine. They are strong plants. But how are my campers doing?"

"My stomach hurts," said Lucy Puppy, "and my heart hurts too." Lucy Bunny's face felt hot, and her muscles were tight.

"Those are emotions," said the gopher. "They happen in your mind and body." He pulled out a piece of paper with some pictures: happy, sad, angry, afraid.

Lucy Puppy suddenly knew why her stomach hurt. "I'm sad," she said.

"I'm angry!" said Lucy Bunny.

"Yes," said the gopher. "Everyone has emotions. Naming them helps us feel better!"

QUESTIONS:

Lucy Puppy's stomach hurt when she felt sad. Lucy Bunny felt hot when she got angry.

- ➡ Where in your body do you feel sad?
- ➡ Where in your body do you feel angry?
- ➡ Where in your body do you feel afraid?
- ➡ Where in your body do you feel happy?

ACTIVITY:
Name Your Funny-Bunny Emotions

We all have emotions!

Some of our emotions feel good: happy, excited, brave.

Some of our emotions are harder: angry, sad, afraid.

Naming emotions helps us make the emotion more peaceful.

Naming emotions helps us think more clearly.

Naming emotions helps us tell other people how we are feeling.

Notice the feelings in your body and write down what you are feeling right now.

For example, "I feel **angry**."

....

....

....

....

Around the Campfire

The two Lucys and the gopher mended the basil patch. The sky was growing dark, and they smelled smoke from the campfire. It was story time!

Lucy Puppy's dad stood by the fire in front of the scouts. "My name is Sebastian, and I have a story to tell," he said. The campers grew quiet. "This is the story of the bear and the bees."

Sebastian Bear told them about the time he bravely fought 500 bees just to get one pot of honey. He proudly showed the pot to the scouts, when—*buzz buzz!*—a bee landed right on his nose.

"Help! Help!" he cried, waving his arms in the air. The honey pot flew out of his paws and landed upside down on his big furry head. Sebastian shook his ears in surprise, and everyone laughed together.

Lucy Bunny smiled as she made a s'more and topped it with a carrot. She thought about all she had learned and took a slow, mindful bite. Like in the Animal Crackers game, this mindful bite made it easier for Lucy Bunny to sit quietly on the log by the fire.

QUESTIONS:

➡ Sebastian Bear is brave and silly. When was a time you were brave? When was a time you were silly?

➡ Lucy Bunny likes to eat s'mores topped with a carrot. Have you invented any new food ideas? What are they?

➡ Lucy Bunny loves carrots. What is your favorite food?

ACTIVITY: Build Your Own S'mores

A s'more is like a sandwich, but it is usually made with graham crackers for bread and filled with a roasted marshmallow and chocolate. Would you like to design your own s'mores? Lucy Bunny put a carrot on her s'more. Draw your own s'mores in the picture.

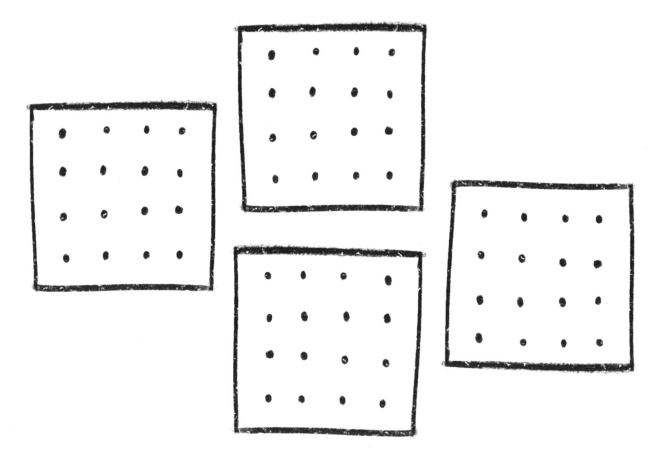

The Special Journal

When the fire grew small and the stars appeared, it was time to go. Lucy Puppy and Lucy Bunny hugged each other. "Goodbye, Lucy," they both said. "See you soon!"

Lucy Bunny's parents arrived with her brothers and sisters to take her home, and they hopped together down the path.

"Did you have fun?" her dad asked.

Lucy happily told them about the dance party, the basil patch, and, most important, all about Lucy Puppy and Sebastian Bear. Her little brother could not stop giggling when she acted out the honey pot landing on Sebastian Bear's head.

That night Lucy Bunny curled in bed next to her siblings, snug and warm. Her mind was filled with thoughts of the day, and Lucy Bunny could not sleep. She had a special journal for these restless nights. Lucy Bunny opened the journal and drew animal crackers and the basil patch, thinking of its green leaves and spicy smell. She remembered the warm sun on her fur as she drew it and remembered the fire crackling in the night air as she colored the campfire.

Lucy Bunny named her emotions. She felt happy, cozy, and loved.

QUESTIONS:

→ Lucy's dad and siblings made sure she got home safely. What nice things does your family do for you?

→ When Lucy can't sleep, she draws in her journal. What do you do when you can't sleep?

→ Lucy named her emotions. She feels happy, cozy, and loved. How do you feel?

ACTIVITY: Keep a Journal

You can keep a journal, just like Lucy Bunny, for drawing, decoration, or writing stories. Try these things in your journal:

⊙ Draw pictures or write about your day.
⊙ Every night, write or draw about what made you feel happy.
⊙ Glue in pictures of places you want to visit or anything else you are dreaming about.
⊙ Create a collage of words or pictures that show special things about you.

BILLIE JEAN, the DRAMA QUEEN?

Billie Jean's Morning Routine

Billie Jean Chihuahua loved getting ready for school. She carefully combed her fur and brushed her teeth. She planned to wear her red sweater from Le Bon Marche in Paris and painted her nails bright pink. Billie Jean smiled as she pranced in front of the mirror.

Billie Jean loved reading and writing. She especially loved her teacher, Ms. Berry, who everyone knew was the nicest teacher in the third grade. Still, her belly hurt a little as she thought about her schoolwork.

No one knew that Billie Jean worried about doing well in school. She was always losing her pencils, she was often late for class, and she repeatedly forgot things at home, like her homework and lunch bag. Sometimes her teacher needed to remind her of what they were doing in class. Billie Jean had such a hard time that she started wearing sunglasses in second grade so no one could see when she wasn't paying attention.

She took a breath, turned on her PawPad, and searched for "puppy yoga." Piper Puppy's video reassured her that stretching would help her be calm and focused. Billie Jean hoped she was right!

QUESTIONS:

➔ Billie Jean has mixed feelings about school. What do you love about school? Is there anything you worry about?

➔ Ms. Berry is the nicest teacher in the third grade. What are some nice things about your teacher?

➔ Did you ever forget your homework? Do you ever have trouble paying attention? Do you sometimes need a reminder?

ACTIVITY: Puppy Yoga Stretches

Start out on your hands and knees.

Walk your hands forward one step.

Push your hips back so your rear is over your heels, and push your hands forward until your head touches the floor. Keep your arms stretched, elbows off the floor, and curl your toes under. This position is called Puppy Pose.

Stretch out your fingertips and take a few deep breaths, letting all of your muscles stretch and relax.

Paris . . .

Billie Jean felt great after puppy yoga. She opened her closet full of sweaters and ribbons that her grandma had bought her from the fashionable shops in Paris. Billie Jean chose a glittery red bow that sparkled and shone just like the lights she had seen on the Eiffel Tower. What a wonderful day that had been! Billie Jean and her grandma had listened to live music by the River Seine. They shared chocolates and cheeses and ate an entire baguette together.

Billie Jean missed her grandma. She decided to draw a picture of herself and her grandma together in Paris and gathered paper and some crayons. Big brown Eiffel Tower. Beautiful blue sky. Grandma in her pink dress. Where was that pink crayon? Hmm . . . it wasn't in the box. Billie Jean knew she had seen it yesterday.

Oh, it was sitting next to her schoolbooks. Oh no! Seeing her schoolbooks helped Billie Jean remember that she had been getting ready for school. She looked at the time. She was late again! She grabbed her sunglasses and ran out the door.

➡ Billie Jean has a special relationship with her grandma. Who is special to you in your family? What do you like to do together?

➡ Billie Jean was so busy thinking about her grandma that she forgot to get ready for school. Do your thoughts or daydreams make you late sometimes?

ACTIVITY:
Color in Billie Jean's Sweaters

Billie Jean likes to color. Coloring is creative and fun! Coloring helps us be in the present moment and have calm focus.

Try coloring Billie Jean's sweaters. Her favorite color is red, but you can use any color or pattern you choose.

A Stroll Down Main Street

Billie Jean hurried outside and rushed down Main Street to get to school. She was late, and she wanted to move quickly.

The sun was bright yellow, the sky was clear blue, and Billie Jean took a deep breath of the fresh air. Her running paws made a *pitter patter* sound on the sidewalk as buses and cars passed her by. She smelled fresh-cut grass, bluebonnets, and daisies. Billie Jean slowed down just long enough to explore how soft the flower petals felt on her nose. A beautiful monarch butterfly caught her eye, and she followed it along the path as it fluttered from flower to flower. Behind her sunglasses, Billie Jean saw squirrels scampering up a big tree, passing a nest holding three little birds.

The more Billie Jean saw, the less she hurried. In fact, she felt perfectly content to enjoy her stroll down Main Street. Billie Jean forgot about the time and did not worry about school, and her belly did not hurt at all. She felt happy and calm. It was lovely!

QUESTIONS:

→ Billie Jean noticed so much on her walk that she didn't think about anything else. What activities keep your full attention? Circle your answers.

> Coloring? Yes / No

> Reading? Yes / No

> Baking? Yes / No

> Playing sports? Yes / No

> Swimming? Yes / No

> Riding your bicycle? Yes / No

→ What other activities hold your attention?

....

....

....

....

ACTIVITY:
Take Yourself Out
for a Walk

Do you want to walk mindfully like Billie Jean? Just take a grown-up along and step outside! What do you notice?

Is it hot or cold? Is it day or night?

Can you name five things you see?

Can you name four things you hear?

Can you name three things you can touch?

Can you name two things you smell?

Is there anything you taste?

The Drama Queen

Billie Jean arrived at puppy school just as the class was taking out their math homework. She ran to her seat and pulled her worksheet out of her bag, spilling crumpled papers, broken pencils, and a few day-old biscuits on the floor. Billie Jean blushed as she hurried to clean up the mess. Beside her, Julia Pug pretended to put on sunglasses and whispered, "What a drama queen!" to Sienna Schnauzer, who giggled.

Billie Jean pretended to ignore her. Julia Pug was always making fun of other puppies. Last weekend, Julia made fun of Billie Jean at Tanner the Labrador's birthday party. She said Billie Jean was rude not to sing "Happy Birthday." Billie Jean wasn't trying to be rude, but the cookies on the table looked so yummy that she just had to take a bite—and who could sing while eating?

"Billie Jean? Please can you tell us the answer to number 10?"

Billie Jean was startled out of her thoughts by Ms. Berry's question. She had to think fast! Billie Jean took three slow breaths to concentrate. The answer to number 10 was 14 apples.

ACTIVITY:
Follow Your Puppy Breath

Find a quiet place to sit. Close your eyes.

Relax and breathe naturally. Place your hand on your belly and feel your belly rise and fall as you breathe, just like a wave on the ocean.

Imagine following your breath along its path. Follow your breath as it enters your body from the tip of your nose and travels down to your belly button. Then follow your breath back up again. In and out, from nose to belly button, and back again. Back and forth.

Learning about Ms. Berry

Ms. Berry finished going over the homework and asked the puppies to line up for a walk to the library.

"Billie Jean," she said with a kind smile, "please stay here with me for a moment."

Billie Jean felt nervous. Had she done something wrong?

Ms. Berry invited Billie Jean to sit at her large desk. She pulled out a piece of paper and drew four lines in a crisscross pattern. "Would you like to play tic-tac-paw?"

Billie Jean loved tic-tac-paw! They played together while Ms. Berry asked about her pretty bow and Billie Jean told her all about Paris.

"You are very smart," said Ms. Berry, "and very kind. I wonder if you sometimes struggle to listen or focus."

Billie Jean took off her sunglasses and stared at her teacher in surprise. "I do," she said. "Are you mad at me?"

"Not at all," said Ms. Berry. "I have a hard time focusing too."

"You do?" asked Billie Jean.

"Yes," said Ms. Berry. "Even though I am smart and very creative, there are certain things I have to work extra hard at, like paying attention and staying organized."

"Really?" asked Billie Jean.

"Yes!" said Ms. Berry. "Everyone is good at some things and has a harder time with other things. For example, I am a great teacher but not a very good basketball player."

Billie Jean laughed.

Ms. Berry continued. "You are great at reading and writing. You play tic-tac-paw very well. You have a harder time with focusing. Now that I know, maybe I can help."

QUESTIONS:

➡ Everyone has their strengths and weaknesses. Billie Jean is great at reading, writing, and tic-tac-paw. She has a hard time with focusing, organizing her bag, and being on time. What are you great at?

➡ What is harder for you to do?

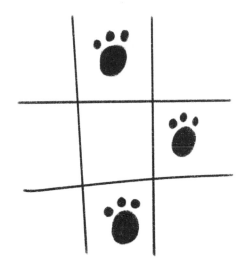

ACTIVITY: Tic-Tac-Paw

Play a game of tic-tac-paw! You will need a friend or a grown-up to play with. Choose who will be X and who will be paw. The winner is the first to get three Xs or three paws in a row, going vertically, horizontally, or diagonally. If no one gets three in a row, it's a tie! Try again!

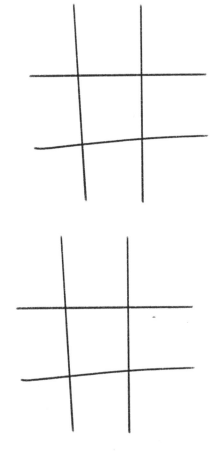

Ms. Berry's Tricks

Over the next few days, Ms. Berry was a big help to Billie Jean. She invited Billie Jean to sit closer to the chalkboard. She helped Billie Jean color-code her homework and put a smiley face on her desk when she paid attention the correct way. If Ms. Berry saw that Billie Jean was struggling to sit still, she let her take the mail to the office to let her move her puppy body around a little.

Ms. Berry made time each day in class for cleaning out bookbags and gave everyone a special pad to write their homework in. She even taught the class a trick where they could use their water bowls to calm down when their emotions became big or bothersome.

Now that it was easier to focus, Billie Jean was learning so many new things. She discovered the best way to bury her bone, practiced proper barking etiquette, and watched a video about dogs helping human police. Billie Jean was feeling more confident and planned to try something new. As the class moved outside for recess, Billie Jean took a moment to calm her emotions using the water bowl trick.

QUESTIONS:

→ Sometimes Billie Jean's emotions become too big or bothersome. What does that mean? Do you ever feel that way?

→ Ms. Berry helped Billie Jean in so many ways. How does your teacher help students in your class?

→ Have you ever been nervous about trying something new?

ACTIVITY: Emotions Water Bowl

Fill a bowl with icy cold water. Look at the water. Notice how clear it is. Touch the surface lightly with your fingertip. Lift your finger and watch the drops of water fall back into the bowl.

Stare into the bowl and notice any emotions you are feeling: happy, sad, frustrated, peaceful, and so forth. Imagine each emotion like a bubble in the water. As you feel each one, imagine that you watch it form in the water, rise to the top of the bowl, and float away.

When you are ready, finish by splashing a little cold water on your face. Refreshing!

Billie Jean, the *All-Star?*

Billie Jean wanted to play baseball at recess. She loved to play with her cousins, but at school she always hid behind her sunglasses. Who could throw and catch with giant sunglasses on? Billie Jean made a big, brave choice. She took off her sunglasses, left them in her cubby, and went out to recess.

The coach put her on the blue team and let her try pitching. Julia Pug smiled when Barkley Dalmatian stepped up to the plate.

"Easy home run, Barkley!" yelled Julia.

The playground grew quiet, and all eyes were on Billie Jean. They watched in amazement as she wound the ball up and threw a perfect pitch.

"Strike one!" yelled the umpire.

Barkley looked surprised. He swung hard on the next pitch.

"Strike two!"

Barkley had his eyes on the ball as he choked up on the bat for the third pitch.

"Strike three!"

Billie Jean's team was cheering, but Barkley looked sad. Billie Jean trotted over to him and gave him a high five and a smile.

"That was a great try," she said.

"Thanks!" said Barkley. "I didn't know you liked baseball. Do you want to come to my baseball birthday next weekend?"

"Yes!" said Billie Jean.

QUESTIONS:

→ Billie Jean made a big, brave choice to put down her sunglasses. Why do you think her choice was brave?

→ Have you ever made a big, brave choice? What was it?

→ Billie Jean did not cheer when Barkley struck out. Do you think that was the right choice?

ACTIVITY:
Share Happiness to Grow Happiness

Find a comfortable sitting position and close your eyes. Think about how everyone experiences lots of different feelings.

Imagine someone who you are close to, such as an adult, sibling, or friend. How do they look when they are happy? How do they act? How do they sound? Do they act differently when they are happy than when they are sad or angry?

Now make a kind wish and send it their way. Imagine them being happy. How does that make you feel? Can you do something that will make them happy? Give it a try!

A Present for Barkley

Billie Jean looked through her closet for something special to wear to Barkley's birthday party. She left her sunglasses lying neatly in the drawer and chose a pink sweater, a black velvet bow with ruby sparkles, and earrings shaped like little Eiffel Towers.

Knock knock! "Billie Jean, we need to leave in 15 minutes." Her mom came into the room and sat beside her. "Well, don't you look pretty! That bow brings out the sparkle in your eyes."

Billy Jean smiled and spun around so her mother could see the full effect.

"What have you gotten Barkley for a present?" her mom asked.

"Oh no!" cried Billie Jean. She had forgotten all about a present.

"It's okay," her mom said. "I have a great idea."

Billie Jean's mom pulled out a square of fancy blue paper. She showed Billie Jean how origami lets you fold paper to create beautiful objects. When her mom was done, the paper looked just like a little dog. Billie Jean's mom helped her tuck a cookie inside. What a fun surprise!

"Sometimes the problem caused by forgetting to plan simply requires a creative solution," said Billie Jean's mom with a smile.

QUESTIONS:

- Billie Jean forgot to get Barkley a present. Do you remember a time when you forgot something? What was it, and how did you solve the problem it created?

- Billie Jean's mom showed her that creativity can solve problems. What does it mean to be creative? How are you creative?

ACTIVITY:
Origami Surprise!

1. Start with a square sheet of paper and lay it on a table with a corner at the top. Fold it in half so the top corner meets the bottom corner.

2. Make a crease by folding it in half so the left corner meets the right corner. Unfold it.

3. Fold the left corner down along the dotted line to form an ear. Repeat on the right side.

4. Fold the bottom corner up along the dotted line.

5. Draw eyes and a nose.

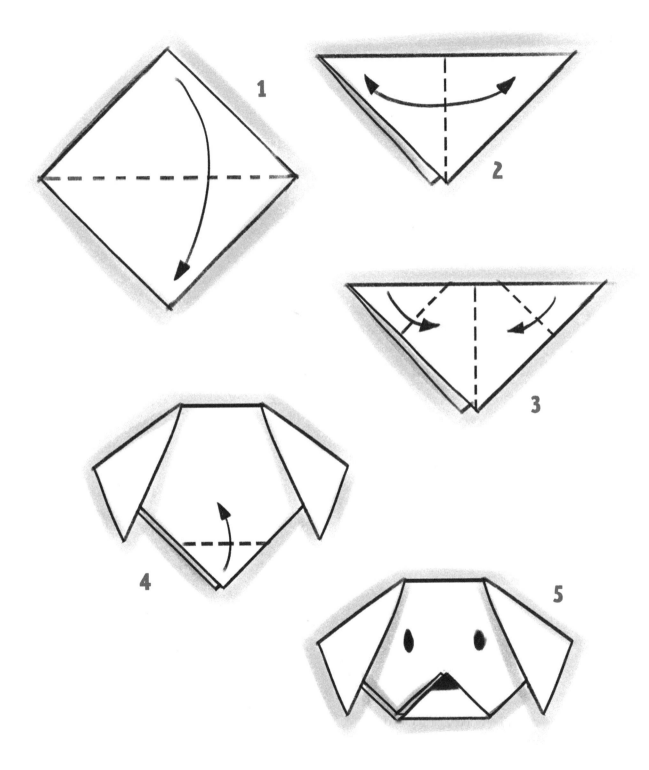

The Birthday Party

When Billie Jean arrived at the party, Barkley bowled her over with a big friendly greeting. She was surprised and delighted that the others seemed happy to see her too. Josh Rottweiler tossed her a cookie from across the room, the Pekingese twins admired her pink sweater, and Maeley the Silky Terrier invited her to dinner next week.

Everyone went out to Barkley's backyard to play baseball. Barkley chose Billie Jean to be on his team, and when she hit a pop fly to left field (easily caught by Josh Rottweiler), no one seemed mad. Even Julia Pug said, "Nice try, Billie Jean."

After the game, Barkley's dad brought out a big cake made of chicken and rice! Billie Jean sat between Sienna and Maeley, and they chatted about music and baseball while they ate. When Barkley opened Billie Jean's present, he seemed pleased, and the other pups were impressed. Billie Jean felt happy. She thought of all the things she was thankful for in her head: delicious cake, baseball games, trips to Paris, new friends, and most of all her family and Ms. Berry, who loved her and made her feel special.

QUESTIONS:

➡ Can you name three things that Billie Jean did to have fun at the party?

➡ Barkley's cake was made of his favorite foods: chicken and rice. If you had a cake made of your favorite foods, what kind of cake would it be?

ACTIVITY: Gratitude Journaling

Write about at least three things that you feel thankful for today. You can also use the space to draw pictures or create a collage to express your gratitude.

Repeat this activity in a blank notebook or pad of paper every day for a week and see how it makes you feel. If you like it, keep it going!

A Happy Ending

When the party ended, Maeley gave Billie Jean her phone number so they could plan their dinner. Barkley high-fived her and gave everyone a bone to take home. Billie Jean was so happy! She ran to her mom's car to tell her all about the party.

"I was on Barkley's team!" she gushed. "And I hit a pop fly that got caught, but no one cared, Mom, and I pitched three perfect strikes. Did you know I could do that?"

Billie Jean's mom laughed.

"We had a cake made of rice and chicken, and Sienna likes to dance, and I'm going to dinner at Maeley's house next weekend!"

"Billie Jean!" her mom said. "You are talking too fast for me to understand."

Billie Jean wanted her mom to understand how amazing the party was and how happy she felt, but she had to slow down first. She stopped talking to let her body wiggle and her tail wag until she was ready. Now she could speak more slowly.

"Okay, Mom," she said with a big smile, "it all started when Barkley opened the door . . ."

ACTIVITY: Wag Your Tail

Stand up straight and tall.

Bend your arms at the elbow and make a gentle fist with each hand.

Think happy thoughts and notice what happens to your body. Does the excitement make you want to wag your "tail"?

Wiggle your hips and swing your arms from side to side!

The happier you feel, the faster you wiggle and swing.

Move faster and faster until you are ready to stop!

Then take a deep breath and relax!

The Characters Talk about ADHD

Fig the Bird

What was your favorite part of your story?
When I met my best friend, Fern.

How does ADHD make you feel?
It makes me feel fast! I fly fast, think fast, and speak fast! Sometimes I am too fast and have to slow myself down.

Do you have a favorite method to use?
Feather flutter! It's easy when you're covered in feathers. I also love spotting bugs in the Forest Name Game.

How does having ADHD make you feel special?
Everyone with ADHD is different. I am special because I have lots of energy and I am always ready for fun.

If you could give the reader some advice, what would it be?
Be proud of who you are!

Fern the Fox

What was your favorite part of your story?
When we found the wild berries.

How does ADHD make you feel?
Sometimes my thoughts are very big or interesting, and it is hard to listen to other people.

Do you have a favorite method to use?
I like Wiggle and Freeze and also Silent as a Fox.

How does having ADHD make you feel special?
Having ADHD helps me have a great imagination!

If you could give the reader some advice, what would it be?
When you are walking in the forest, don't think about bugs!

Lucy Puppy

What was your favorite part of your story?
When we dug holes for the herb garden. That was so much fun!

How does ADHD make you feel?
I have a lot of energy! I like to move around, and I don't like to be bored.

Do you have a favorite method?
Naming emotions always makes me feel a lot better.

How does having ADHD make you feel special?
I think it helps me have a big heart.

If you could give the reader some advice, what would it be?
Be a good scout!

Lucy Bunny

What was your favorite part of the story?
When we all danced to DJ Draper!

How does ADHD make you feel?
Sometimes it makes me feel shy when I don't want other animals to see me wiggling, but mostly I feel just the same as everyone else.

Do you have a favorite method to use?
Animal Crackers is my favorite. Do you know it also works with carrots?

How does having ADHD make you feel special?
It's another way that I am like my best friend, Lucy Puppy.

If you could give the reader some advice, what would it be?
Try new things and never give up!

Billie Jean Chihuahua

What was your favorite part of your story?
When I put down my sunglasses and got to play ball!

How does ADHD make you feel?
I feel embarrassed when I lose attention or act differently. Sometimes I know what I'm supposed to do, but I still can't do it.

Do you have a favorite method to use?
Coloring mindfully about Paris helps me feel calmer and happier! So does following my puppy breath when I need to keep my cool!

How does having ADHD make you feel special?
Having ADHD helped me get to know my teacher better and be brave.

If you could give the reader some advice, what would it be?
Talk to a grown-up and ask for help when you need it!

YOU ARE IN CHARGE!

It's time to bring the mindfulness practices we learned into our own lives. Like learning to play basketball or the piano, it's important to practice every day to develop your skills. In this section, you'll have a chance to practice with a few examples from each story to get you started. At the end of this chapter is a special place where you can help teach mindfulness to your favorite grown-ups . . . and even quiz them too!

Practice Mindfulness at Home

Let's talk about how mindfulness activities helped the animals and how you can try it at home. Fig is a bright little bird whose mind is very active and excited. Mindfulness helps calm his mind and clear his thoughts. Fern is Fig's kind best friend who wants to pay attention but is very easily distracted. Mindfulness helps her listen and bring her thoughts into focus. Lucy Bunny is an awesome dancer, but once she starts, it's so hard to stop. Her ears keep twitching and her foot keeps thumping long after the music stops. Mindfulness relaxes all of her muscles so her body can feel calm. Lucy Puppy is full of energy and feels all of her emotions very strongly. Mindfulness calms her happy, sad, angry, and worried feelings so she can feel peaceful. Billie Jean is a super cool Chihuahua who daydreams, is forgetful, and runs late. Mindfulness helps her focus, remember, and keep moving along.

Now that we know how mindfulness helped our animal friends, it's time to think about how mindfulness activities can help you! All of the activities in the book can be used at home, outside, in school, and in lots of other places. Let's practice a few of our animal friends' favorites.

FIG'S FAVORITE: Forest Name Game

Fig and Fern play the **Forest Name Game** (page 10) when Fern starts daydreaming and has a hard time listening and paying attention. This game helps us come back to the present moment and notice what is happening. It improves our focus and reminds us to continue with our tasks.

→ **Do you ever have trouble getting things done at home because your mind starts wandering?** Are there ever times when grown-ups have to remind you to do things like get dressed or eat your breakfast even when you are trying your very best? This happens to lots of kids. The Forest Name Game can help.

→ **At school, do you have any subjects that are harder to focus on?** Think about subjects that might be hard for you or that you don't find very interesting. Some clues that your mind is wandering in school may be that you are having a hard time listening to your teacher. Has that ever happened to you? Doing the Forest Name Game silently can help.

→ **What if you are playing baseball and you are getting bored in the outfield?** Practicing the Forest Name Game can help remind you of where you are and what is important for you to do right now.

Write down times when you would like to try out Fig's trick to stay focused.

....

....

....

....

....

FERN'S FAVORITE: Silent as a Fox

Fern and Fig were so distracted by everything in the forest it was hard to remember where they had seen the wild berries. They used **Silent as a Fox** (page 25) to clear their minds and help them remember. Silent as a Fox can help you remember something important. It can also be used to simply clear your mind for a calm, peaceful feeling.

- ➔ **Have you ever lost anything that was important to you?** For instance, have you ever misplaced the homework you did only last night? Before you look all over the house, try Silent as a Fox and see if you can remember where it is.

- ➔ **Perhaps you lose little things.** For instance, lots of kids lose their shoes. Silent as a Fox can help you visualize where you left your shoes and help you find them.

- ➔ **Do you ever find your mind racing with a lot of thoughts?** Perhaps you can't stop thinking about an exciting event that is coming up, your mind is trying to work out the answer to a puzzle, or you keep thinking about something over and over. Silent as a Fox can help you clear your mind and blow away thoughts that are bugging you.

Write down times that you would like to try Fern's trick to help you remember something or make your mind clear and peaceful.

....

....

....

....

FERN'S OTHER FAVORITE: Wiggle and Freeze

Now that Fig and Fern have learned to **Wiggle and Freeze** (page 16), they love to have fun with it! Fig especially likes to try it when his body feels full of energy and it's hard to sit still. Do you ever feel like you need to get the wiggles out like Fig?

→ **Has it ever been hard for you to sit still while you are reading a book or playing a board game?** Sometimes our body is the wiggliest when we are supposed to be sitting still. A game of Wiggle and Freeze before these activities may make it easier to sit.

→ **Do you ever need to wait for grown-ups to help you with something, or wait for your friend to come over to play? Maybe you are waiting with your parents on a long line at the store.** Another thing a lot of kids find hard to do is wait. Waiting can fill us with wiggles! A quiet game of Wiggle and Freeze can help get those wiggles out.

→ **Our bodies can become especially full of wiggles at bedtime.** A game of Wiggle and Freeze can help us get the wiggles and the giggles out before bed so that our bodies can relax and sleep.

Write down times that you can use Wiggle and Freeze to get the wiggles out.

....

....

....

....

....

LUCY BUNNY'S FAVORITE: Animal Crackers

Lucy Bunny used the **Animal Crackers** activity (page 48) to calm her body when she was having trouble keeping her paws, ears, and nose still. Eating mindfully gives us something to do with our hands and mouth and may help other parts of our body remain still and calm. As a bonus, it helps us feel peaceful and pay attention to a bite of delicious food!

⊙ **Are you ever offered food at a place that is busy or exciting, like a birthday party?** Eating your first bite or two of food mindfully like Lucy Bunny may help your body sit still after running or jumping around.

⊙ **Do you ever have a hard time waiting for your friends or family to finish eating at the dinner table?** Try eating the last few bites of your food mindfully. It will make your meal last longer and help your body be still and quiet while you wait for others to finish up.

⊙ **Does your body tend to fidget and move a lot in school when you are sitting at your desk or your table?** If you are allowed, try keeping a few small snacks with you. You can place them in your mouth quietly a few times per day and eat them slowly and mindfully while you listen to your teacher. If you are not allowed, try drinking a few sips of cool water mindfully when you wish to calm your muscles and refresh your attention.

Write down times that you wish to calm your body and eat mindfully.

....

....

....

....

LUCY PUPPY'S FAVORITE:
Name Your Funny-Bunny Emotions

Lucy Bunny and Lucy Puppy felt better when they noticed the feelings in their bodies and gave them a name in **Name Your Funny-Bunny Emotions** (page 57). Everyone has emotions! Sometimes emotions can get very big, and it is helpful to name them out loud.

→ **Have you ever felt so happy and excited that it was hard to sit still?** Some kids have such a hard time staying still when they feel happy that they may get in trouble for silly things they would not normally do, like jumping on the couch, running around, or knocking things over. If that happens to you, try to name your emotions.

→ **Can you remember a time you acted out because you felt angry?** This happens to a lot of kids. Sometimes you may not be ready to explain why you feel angry, but naming your emotion may help you feel better. Share it with your mom, dad, or any other grown-up who is there to help you.

→ **Do you know what *embarrassment* means?** It is one of the hardest feelings to share. Try discussing it with a grown-up. Talk about how it feels in your body and then try naming it the next time you feel it. It may be hard to believe, but everyone feels embarrassed sometimes!

Write down times that you wish to name your emotions.

....

....

....

....

BILLIE JEAN'S FAVORITE:
Follow Your Puppy Breath

Billie Jean used **Follow Your Puppy Breath** (page 78) when she felt anxious about arriving late for school and having to answer a question about the homework. Anxiety is a normal feeling that happens in your body when you are worried or stressed. It might make your muscles feel tense, cause your heart to race, or make it hard to think clearly. Following your puppy breath helps you take deep, slow breaths to feel more peaceful and more focused.

→ **Can you think of times when you have felt stressed or anxious?** Perhaps when you were running late for school or for an activity? When you are worried about being late, it can make it harder to find the things you need to get going. Following your puppy breath can help.

→ **Are there days when you have a lot to do?** Maybe you have a lot of homework, but you also have chores to do. If you start to feel anxious or stressed, following your puppy breath is a great trick to try.

→ **Do you feel overwhelmed in big, noisy places like the supermarket?** This is another great example where following your puppy breath can help.

Write down times when you would like to try Billie Jean's trick for calming your body and your mind.

....

....

....

....

Homework . . . for Your Grown-Ups

Have you ever wanted to give homework to the grown-ups in your life? Great! Here is a fun way you can teach them what you have learned and put them to the test!

Ask them to schedule some special time with you. At your scheduled time, sit down with them and give them a piece of paper and a pencil. Read them your top three favorite activities from this book and teach them how to do them. You may need to teach them a few times. Grown-ups sometimes need extra help!

Ask them to take notes. Give them a little time to practice!

Then sit down and ask them to demonstrate to you the three activities you taught them.

After the demonstration, complete the following report card together by taking turns answering these questions.

1. **What did you like most about the activities?**

Name:	Name:

2. Did the activities help you feel calm?

Name:	Name:
· ·	· ·
· ·	· ·
· ·	· ·
· ·	· ·
· ·	· ·
· ·	· ·

3. Did you struggle with any of the activities?

Name:	Name:
· ·	· ·
· ·	· ·
· ·	· ·
· ·	· ·
· ·	· ·
· ·	· ·

4. **Is there any activity that you would change?**
   How would you change it?

Name:	Name:
....	....
....	....
....	....
....	....
....	....

5. **Which activities would you like to do again?**

Name:	Name:
....	....
....	....
....	....
....	....
....	....

Resources

Books

The Family ADHD Solution: A Scientific Approach to Maximizing Your Child's Attention and Minimizing Parental Stress, by Mark Bertin (2011)

Good Enough to Eat: A Kid's Guide to Food and Nutrition, by Lizzy Rockwell (2009)

A Handful of Quiet: Happiness in Four Pebbles, by Thich Nhat Hanh (2008)

Mindful Parenting for ADHD: A Guide to Cultivating Calm, Reducing Stress, and Helping Children Thrive, by Mark Bertin (2015)

Neurofeedback 101: Rewiring the Brain for ADHD, Anxiety, Depression and Beyond (without Medication), by Michael P. Cohen (2020)

Smart but Scattered: The Revolutionary "Executive Skills" Approach to Helping Kids Reach Their Potential, by Peg Dawson and Richard Guare (2009)

What Your ADHD Child Wishes You Knew: Working Together to Empower Kids for Success in School and Life, by Sharon Saline (2018)

Websites

ADDitude: Inside the ADHD Mind
A magazine with articles, webinars, and podcasts relevant to ADHD.
⊕ *ADDitudeMag.com*

American Psychological Association Psychologist Locator
Find a psychologist in your area to provide an ADHD assessment or intervention.
⊕ *locator.APA.org*

Children and Adults with Attention-Deficit/Hyperactivity Disorder (CHADD)
CHADD is a great resource for ADHD education, support, and advocacy.
⊕ *CHADD.org*

National Institute of Mental Health
Research and statistics, opportunities to join clinical studies, free brochures, and shareable resources.
⊕ *NIMH.NIH.gov/health/topics/attention-deficit-hyperactivity
-disorder-adhd/index.shtml*

Psychology Today
Find a therapist specializing in ADHD in your area.
⊕ *PsychologyToday.com*

Index

About the Author

 SHARON GRAND, PhD, is a licensed psychologist who is professionally and personally very familiar with ADHD. She completed her doctorate at Auburn University in Alabama and then returned to her home in New York to complete her internship in psychology and a postdoctoral fellowship in neuropsychology and rehabilitation. Dr. Grand has worked with families and children for many years and now owns Wavelengths Psychology and Neurofeedback, a private group practice on Long Island. She is fortunate to have an awesome team of therapists dedicated to a mind-brain-body approach to resilience and mental health. Dr. Grand loves working with children and especially loves books and reading stories together. She appreciates time spent with her son, her husband, her family, and her friends and enjoys doing lots of things she is not very good at, including baking, singing, and dancing. Dr. Grand loves mindfulness because it helps her remember to let go of the little things and have fun!

About the Illustrator

 TAIA MORLEY is an illustrator and author whose work has appeared in a variety of children's books, magazines, toys, and even a bookmobile! She carries a sketchbook wherever she goes because there is always something interesting to draw. You can visit her online at TaiaMorley.com and @taiamorley on Instagram.

CPSIA information can be obtained
at www.ICGtesting.com
Printed in the USA
JSHW051954141021
19551JS00006B/18